# HEAVENLY VISITATION

## A Guide to Participating in the Supernatural

KEVIN L. ZADAI

HEAVENLY VISITATION
*A Guide to Participating in the Supernatural*
by Kevin L. Zadai

Printed in the United States of America.

ISBN 9781498430845

www.xulonpress.com

# Table of Contents

# Foreword

What would it be like, while suspended on the outer frontier of physical death, to visit with Jesus and have Him reveal the eternal purpose and deeper meaning of your life? You'll soon learn it firsthand from my good friend Kevin Zadai in his book Heavenly Visitation: A Guide to Participating in the Supernatural. In these pages, you'll shortly discover that God doesn't evaluate or compare your success with what many others consider to be noteworthy achievements, but simply by your faithfulness to do what He asks you to do while on earth.

You've heard it said that integrity is what you do when no one is watching. Well, someone is always watching, and in His eyes even a sparrow has so much importance that He knows when it falls to the ground. This book will teach you that in obeying whatever He asks you to do for even the seemingly insignificant sparrow, you are a success in His eyes. Heavenly Visitation: A Guide to Participating in the Supernatural is about knowing that in God's eyes the last are first, the servants are the leaders, and the children are those whom the adults should be acting like.

Kevin is on the crest of a new wave of God using ordinary people—people who in the world's eyes are unimportant and doing things that the world considers trivial—to release historic supernatural events. You'll learn how something as seemingly inconsequential as giving a homeless person your lunch could open your eyes to future global economic trends that only God knows.

I've heard Kevin say many times, "I'm a flight attendant who prays in the Spirit. If God can use me, He can use anyone." However, as Kevin knows, being a flight attendant is nothing to apologize for, and he also knows that he's far more than just a flight attendant. That's only his current camouflage. He's one of the sons of God—the kingdom agents—that the earth is groaning to see in full manifestation. He sees angels, has visitations from Jesus, and goes on supernatural adventure missions. In this book, you'll quickly realize that you could do the same and that experiencing the supernatural could become the most natural thing in your life.

Nathanael Wolf
Author of The Gatekeepers

# Author's Note and Special Thanks

I have long anticipated this day—the time when I could share my story with everyone. When the Lord gave me permission to write of my supernatural experience in this book, I began recalling His conversations with me to the best of my ability. This book does not contain a perfect verbatim recount of all of our dialogues; however, it is sufficient to reveal the person of Jesus and His discussions with me to anyone who will listen.

I want to thank everyone who has encouraged me, assisted me, and prayed for me during the writing of this book. A very special thanks to my wife, Kathi, who is the only one who fully understands the spiritual warfare involved with fulfilling this mandate from Jesus. Thank you for your love and commitment to the Lord Jesus and to me. I love you dearly.

Also, a special thanks to Larry Witten and Arline Oliphint for their beautiful job with editing and making the book more readable.

In addition, my special thanks to Dr. Jesse and Cathy Duplantis, Pastors Nathanael and Michelle Wolf, Pastor Don and Christina Priest, Pastor Tom and Kellie Giles, Pastors Massoud and Sarah Sadeghi, and Rev. Ruth Carneal for their spiritual influence and covering over my wife and me. We are eternally thankful.

A special thank you to all our friends, who are too numerous to mention, who surely know how to pray and get things done "in the Spirit."

# Endorsements

When Kevin told me he was going to be writing this book, I was so excited. His experiences with Jesus and the visions that he has had from the Lord need to be given to the body of Christ. Kevin has a word from God for this hour and in this moment for the church. This book is just the beginning of what God has shown him. As you read this book, I hope you are as blessed as I was.

I have had many encounters with people over the years who move strongly in the things of the Spirit. Many of those people are strong in the pulpit, but not so strong in their daily lives. On rare occasion, you meet a man who moves in the things of God all the time. This describes Kevin Zadai. Kevin lives life as a man who knows God. Kevin's connection with the Holy Spirit is demonstrated in even casual conversation. We can be in the middle of a friendly conversation, and he will prophesy exactly what I need to hear at that moment. I am blessed to know him.

Kevin understands how to flow with the Spirit of God in his day-to-day work and life. I have heard countless stories of people touched by on-time words, extemporaneous ministry, and supernatural moves of God through Kevin. His example is one to be followed and looked to.

It can be easy to miss what God is doing in the small things of our daily lives. Kevin knows how to listen intently to God so that he doesn't miss those seemingly insignificant things. God uses them as a catalyst for great revelation.

This is the story of the New Testament church. This is how we all should be living. May this book be an inspiration to those who read it that they too can do mighty things through listening to the voice of God.

Pastor Don Priest

Living Faith Church International

*This book will transform your life!*

I am honored to know Kevin Zadai. His consecration and submission to the calling of God are an inspiration. God has parted many Red Sea experiences to enable him to be a voice to this generation, for such a time is this.

As you read, there will be deposits made into your life that challenge you to make every word count. Proverbs 18:21 says, "Death and life are in the power of the tongue: and they that love it shall eat the fruit thereof." Be ready to look in a mirror and see the changes that must come into your life.

When Kevin opens his mouth, revelation explodes forth with kingdom keys for all ages. As you take to heart the words in this book, you will realize the creative force that is launched each time we move our lips.

Rev. Ruth E. Carneal

Phoenix, Arizona

# Preface

Although the heavenly visitation found in this book happened in 1992, I have not felt that I could speak of it, except to a small group of people, until now. The Bible clearly teaches that there are times and seasons for everything, and I believe this is the season to share this remarkable visitation from Jesus. In the years that followed, I had the privilege of having other heavenly encounters, but they never lasted for the length of time of this initial visit.

The time I spent in the presence of Jesus profoundly changed me to my core. I believe Jesus promised me that my story, including all the things I learned during our conversation, has the capacity to radically change those who read it. It is my prayer that as you read about my vision, you will experience the same thing I experienced and have an even greater outcome.

# Chapter 1

# The End and a Beginning

P eople have asked me if there were prior indications that the supernatural event that occurred to me in the fall of 1992 was about to happen—and there were. Three months prior to the event, I sensed that I was going to pass from earth to heaven. The feeling was so strong that I updated my beneficiaries with my employer of about five years, a major airline. I even told a friend that when I prayed, I sensed that I might be going to heaven soon, and I told her not to be sad if I left. I wasn't afraid to die. In fact, when I thought of dying, I felt an indescribable peace.

I was spending my days working for an airline and my free time doing what I could to help people, especially the poor and homeless. But I was starting to feel somewhat detached from this realm. I felt ready to go; however, it didn't make sense to me that I should die, because I had many productive years of life ahead of me. Even though I was sensing all this, I had no idea what was about to happen.

## AN ELEVATED PERSPECTIVE

We need a new perspective on life because things often look different from a higher vantage point. God wants us to see things from His viewpoint, which is the real one.

*When the Spirit of God takes us to a higher place, revelation comes automatically. From that place of understanding, we can operate in a supernatural way. Although this way of living is natural to God, it seems unnatural to us. However, as we see the purpose for our lives from God's perspective, it is transforming, and the supernatural becomes our new natural.*

In the heavenly realm, freedom, truth, and love prevail, and God has given us access into those realms through Jesus Christ. Although you may find my experience extraordinary, the apostle Paul prayed that it would become ordinary for all Christians to experience the heavenly realm:

The eyes of your understanding being enlightened; that you may know what is the hope of His calling, what are the riches of the glory of His inheritance in the saints.   Ephesians 1:18

[Paul himself] . . . was caught up to Paradise and heard inexpressible words, which it is not lawful for a man to utter.    2 Corinthians 12:4

The apostle John was also caught up in the Spirit and saw things that he recounted in the book of Revelation. He saw future events and wrote about them before they happened. Undoubtedly, the new revelation he received from Jesus Christ changed him.

Although it is hard for us to conceive, the spirit realm is actually more real than the earthly one. The earth is in fact a re-creation of the heavenly realm. However, heaven does not have the hindrances we encounter on earth.

*In heaven there are no restrictions on space and time; things happen very quickly. Colors and sounds are alive and far more enhanced than on earth. The atmosphere around you is full of life. It isn't even necessary to communicate with words because your very thoughts are known.*

## THE OPERATION

I was scheduled to go in for a day surgery to remove my impacted wisdom teeth. They were causing me a lot of pain, so I decided to do the procedure. On the day of my appointment, I was driven to the facility and dropped off and would later be picked up and driven home. In a prep room, I was sedated by an anesthesiologist and then wheeled down a hall to the operating room. I remember being told to count down from one hundred and not getting very far before I was unconscious.

Then I was suddenly outside my body and standing beside the operating table, watching the surgeon and his two female assistants work. When I realized what had happened and that I had passed on, I wanted to inform the doctor. I moved toward him and told him that I had died. However, he did not seem to hear me, so I poked him and spoke louder. He still did not respond, so I went over to one of the nurses and tried to tell her to revive me. It was obvious that no one could hear me, even though I could hear them talking. I could touch and feel them, but they were completely unaware that I was standing next to them. I stepped back to ponder my dilemma. The doctor and nurses did not seem to have any physical evidence that I had died. I was still alive to them.

As I stared at my body on the table, it began to transform into a new, glorified body right before my eyes. Although it had no imperfections, it still looked like me, but it had a brilliance and beauty that resembled an angel of the Lord (see Philippians 3:21). Filled with awe, and without thinking, I said, "I look beautiful!"

The operating room was large, with curtains that could be drawn for privacy and to form four separate rooms to accommodate multiple patients. This day, however, there was no one else in the room except for me, the surgeon, and his assistants; so the curtains were not drawn.

Immediately after my surprised exclamation about the perfection of my body, I heard a man's voice behind me say, "That's what you look like to Me all the time." I turned to see who was speaking to me, and what happened next changed my life forever.

## THE TEACHER ARRIVES

It was Jesus Christ. He was standing on the other side of the room in a white robe. He appeared to be a little less than six feet tall, had beautiful long hair, and His skin was an olive, tan color. His neck and part of a shoulder were exposed by the robe, and I could see that He was muscular.

*At that moment, He was everything to me. He was not just God, but He was my king, commander, savior, brother, and friend.*

As I walked over to Him, He greeted me, and I was aware that He wanted to discuss something very important. As though He knew our time together was limited, without further conversation He immediately began teaching me about the importance of words.

## PASSWORDS TO THE KINGDOM

Jesus began discussing with me the power of words. He emphasized that they are an important key for participation in God's supernatural kingdom. As I stood beside the operating table, beholding my body, He allowed it to remain in its glorified state. Then He approached within about four feet of me, and I was able to see His features more accurately.

He was beautiful in every way. His eyes were clear, full of life, and seemed to contain various colors. He appeared to be thirty to forty years old, and His hair was remarkable.

It was thick and brown, with highlights of different colors, including red and blond, and parted in the middle. It went past his shoulders and down His back and reminded me of a lion's mane. He looked like a handsome king dressed casually.

*He said boldly to me. "In Matthew 12:36, I told My disciples that they would be held accountable for every idle word that came out of their mouths." For a long moment, He just looked at me in silence. Then suddenly He stepped quickly toward me and whispered in my ear, "You know, I meant that!"*

He then stepped back, looked closely at me again, and smiled. I felt His words begin to have an effect on me. I sensed them saturating me as my understanding became enlightened.

Suddenly I realized that He was addressing me in a corrective manner. Feeling convicted in many ways, I immediately made adjustments within myself, realizing that He wanted to help me. Once I made those internal shifts, I was flooded with a new understanding of this truth as scriptures and past experiences cascaded through my mind, confirming and deepening my understanding of His words.

*Either our words are passwords to access God's power to build His kingdom on earth and the purpose He created us for, or they create roadblocks to His purposes.*

I was astonished at how important the words I spoke were. However, that was only the beginning of His teaching. He wanted me (and you) to understand so much more.

# Chapter 2
# ABCs of the Kingdom

J esus' admonishment concerning idle words, followed by His statement, "You know, I meant that!" penetrated deeply into my heart. I was reminded that many of us talk too much, and our babbling gets us in trouble. The Bible says that restraining our words is wise:

> In the multitude of words sin is not lacking, but
> he who restrains his lips is wise.
> Proverbs 10:19

> Even a fool is counted wise when he holds his
> peace; when he shuts his lips, he is considered
> perceptive.                    Proverbs 17:28

## WATCH YOUR WORDS

To settle into who we are in Christ, we must learn to speak only the words that are necessary and constructive for the situation. Titus 2:6 cautions us to be "sober-minded."

*Being sober-minded in your speech means taking the time and making the effort to be aware of every moment and all its implications. Then, if you choose to speak, you can use your words more wisely.*

In Matthew 12:36, Jesus explained, "On the day of judgment men will have to give account for every idle (inoperative, nonworking) word they speak" (AMP).

Rather than speak idle words, we must speak from our spirits (our hearts) and let our *yes* mean "yes" and our *no* mean "no" (see James 5:12). Instead of saying something meaningless, devious, misleading, or manipulative, we must speak truth. By attempting to speak honestly, concisely, and helpfully, we learn to yield to the Holy Spirit within us.

Looking to the Holy Spirit for guidance will make our words more accurate and meaningful, and if we do not know what to say, we will learn to hold our words until we have a better understanding. Replies like, "I need some time to think about that," or "I'm not ready to respond to that at this time" are fair and safe answers.

## FOLLOW THE LEADER

Submitting to authority is another way of remaining sober-minded. We must fully submit to the Word of God and the Holy Spirit, even above our feelings and desires. In addition, the people designated by God to be our pastors and teachers must be allowed to have authority in our lives.

God-given leadership will confirm what heaven is doing and God is speaking in our lives. Remember, above all, the Holy Spirit is here to lead us into all truth (see John 16:13). True submission to authority brings us into a restful state where we are capable of making sound judgments.

## THE FEAR OF THE LORD FALLS

The fear of the Lord will also keep us sober-minded and clear of many harmful situations.

During my college days, I encountered an authentic manifestation of God that created a fear of the Lord. I was seeking God earnestly, praying for hours and fasting at times. My roommate was a Puerto Rican named Angel. We often had good discussions about biblical things, such as the fear of God. However, one evening around nine, we had more than a discussion—we experienced it.

My roommate had often expressed the desire that God use him in the gift of prophecy. I told him that his desire was scriptural and that the apostle Paul expressed the wish that all people would prophesy. First Corinthians 14:1 says,

"Pursue love, and desire spiritual gifts, but especially that you may prophesy."

It was winter and cold outside, so our room's windows were closed. Our dorm rooms were small and usually had two students per room. We studied until nine, and then the halls were opened for visits between students. That night, as we lay on our beds talking about the gift of prophecy, I encouraged my roommate in his desire. Then I noticed something odd. It was becoming windy in our room, and it began to feel warm and very holy. Things were actually blowing around, and yet no windows were open.

All at once, the atmosphere of holiness became so intense that both of us were lying facedown on our beds, confessing every sin we could think of. These confessions spewed out of our mouths as if coming from a machine gun, as we pleaded for forgiveness and mercy. The awesome presence of God continued to become ever stronger and more powerful. Soon I became so overwhelmed that I felt like I might die at any moment.

The fear of God can be a very real thing. The sins I felt compelled to confess had accumulated from the time I was born again up until that moment. We need to keep current accounts with the Lord, according to 1 John 1:7–9:

> But if we walk in the light, as He is in the light, we have fellowship one with another, and the blood of Jesus Christ his Son cleanses us from all sin. If we say that we have no sin, we deceive ourselves, and the truth is not in us. If

we confess our sins, He is faithful and just to forgive us our sins, and to cleanse us from all unrighteousness.

It is important to note that this passage was written to believers *after* they had been born again.

When we finished confessing our sins, I noticed that our beds were making creaking sounds.

*The weight of glory filling that room was powerfully pressing down on our beds and us. It was so holy in that place that at one point I felt as though my body could not take it anymore. I cried out for mercy and heard my roommate doing the same.*

Then I heard footsteps as someone walked into the room to stand between us. I knew it was Jesus, but I could not look into His face because it was so bright and holy around Him. Then it felt as though a furnace door had opened and supernatural heat was flooding our room. As it permeated my entire body, I was aware that it was cleansing me.

I was not able to look up, but I could sense Jesus was leaning over my roommate. He placed His hand on the middle of Angel's back (according to his account), and as the power of God visibly surged through him, he began prophesying. His voice was so loud and forceful that it shook me to the core as his voice reverberated through the room. Jesus spoke to me through my roommate and confirmed my call to ministry. When Angel finished prophesying, Jesus withdrew His hand from him and walked out of the room.

Immediately the room began to calm, the wind died down, and the temperature returned to normal. We continued to lie on our beds for a time, savoring the lingering presence of the Lord. The students who visited us that evening following our heavenly visitation were visibly touched by the presence of God. Some were even brought to tears as they tried to express what they were experiencing. We decided not to tell anyone what had happened to us that night until we finished college. But even after we graduated, we kept it to ourselves for years because the experience was too sacred to put into words and too personal to share.

Whether the fear of God comes to us through a personal visitation, by way of the Holy Spirit, or as He reveals truth through His Word, we can become more like Him every day, learning "the fear of the Lord is the beginning of wisdom" (Psalm 111:10).

## FOUR THINGS GOD HATES

One result of having the fear of the Lord, according to Proverbs 8:13, is to hate evil. In that same verse, God goes on to mention the four things He hates: pride, arrogance, corruption, and perverse speech.

My encounter with Jesus made me aware of the mighty awesomeness of His person. Although we can and should experience His kindness and goodness, we must never forget that He is pure and holy beyond our imagination and not to be taken lightly.

*If we are full of pride or arrogance, we will have to change in order to have fellowship with God because those things are repulsive to Him. All four of the traits mentioned—pride, arrogance, corruption, and perverse speech—create a barrier in our relationship with God.*

When I encountered His awesome presence, it had a humbling effect on me. Because I wanted to know everything that He had to say, I did not want anything hindering my relationship with Him. Jesus gives us the ability to stay away from evil so we can be free of those things that hamper our relationship with Him. We can sense when evil is working and resist it.

His holy presence commands and even demands our respect. We are to love Him and fear Him at the same time. Our fear is not born out of intimidation or dread of being harmed, but out of reverence and respect for Him. We must take responsibility for our lives because we are not our own. He freed us from the ravages of sin at a great price, and our lives now belong to Him (see 1 Corinthians 6:19–20).

## POWER OF THE DOVE

The Spirit of the Lord rested on Jesus all His life from conception onward. It was the Holy Spirit who impregnated

Mary. Jesus submitted to the Holy Spirit, and because of His submission, He had good fruit manifest in His life. We are to do the same:

> And the spirit of the LORD shall rest upon him, the spirit of wisdom and understanding, the spirit of counsel and might, the spirit of knowledge and of the fear of the LORD.; and shall make him of quick understanding in the fear of the LORD: and he shall not judge after the sight of his eyes, neither reprove after the hearing of his ears. Isaiah 11:2–3 KJV

The same Holy Spirit is upon us and within us. All the wonderful attributes mentioned in Isaiah 11:2–3 are available to us. We are no longer of the spirit of this world, which is of the devil, but we have been made one with the Spirit of God. If we are humble and allow His awesome power and presence to manifest within us, He will bring us to victory. Even when we feel weak, after submitting to Him, we can live in power (see 2 Corinthians 13:4). All is attainable, "for in Him we live and move and have our being" (Acts 17:28). Wonderful things are in store for those who fully yield to and trust in Him.

*The Spirit says, "It's time to yield to the overshadowing power of My presence. Don't allow fear of the unknown or the fear of man to keep you from My presence. Only enter in, and you will have your dreams fulfilled. The dreams I gave you for this season will come forth. Do not look to man or his kingdoms, but rather, look to Me and My kingdom, and you will be blessed."*

Remember, God is able to cause you to be successful. Worship Him in holy fear and reverence; bow before Him in humility. Give Him your life, and you can expect an amazing existence. "True humility and fear of the Lord lead to riches, honor, and long life" (Proverbs 22:4 NLT).

## FORMIDABLE DECLARATIONS

*Jesus wants every person on the earth to confess Him as Lord because only through that heartfelt declaration can humanity access the divine covenant with all its benefits and authority.*

Once we have access to God through our belief in Jesus Christ, we can participate in the kingdom of God and begin to grow into our covenant rights and authority through the indwelling of His Spirit. Through revelation, the human spirit can become so saturated in this covenant and its authority that when it speaks out of that revelation, its commands become words backed with the power of Almighty God. As a consequence, the words that come out of our mouths accomplish the intention of His revelation. When they arrive at their destination, a change begins.

Perhaps now you can understand why speaking idle words is forbidden. They are words that have the wrong intention or the wrong destination. Words that don't match your true destination or your true intention should not be uttered. If we knew that every word we said would come true immediately after we spoke it, we would not say a lot of the things we say.

> *The intent of your words has to match their destination, or God considers them idle, or illegal. This is the way words work in the spirit realm. This is what Jesus told me in this vision, and it is what He wants all His children to understand.*

That is why Jesus, in Mark 11: 23–24, taught us to speak to mountains. When a mountain is in your way, it is to be removed. When your intent is to get to God's will on the other side of the mountain, it is your destination; hence the mountain must be removed. A revelation of God's purpose will cause your words to harmonize with where you are going and empower them to get you there. Idle words can hinder God's kingdom from advancing because power words are His way (system) of doing things.

## PROVISIONS OF THE KINGDOM

"But He answered and said, 'It is written, "Man shall not live by bread alone, but by every word that proceeds from the mouth of God"'" (Matthew 4:4).

The Bible says in Mark 1:14 that Jesus came preaching that the kingdom of God was coming. Although you may not have heard much preaching about it, Jesus established God's kingdom on earth with His death for the sins of mankind. Everyone who receives Jesus as their Savior is born (again) into that kingdom. The exciting news is that God has plans for His kingdom to reign over all the earth, and those plans include you.

> *The kingdom of God is in place and advancing, even if we are not presently and actively participating in its progress. Every day we have an opportunity to receive our provision and a "kingdom briefing" from heaven. It comes from our commanding officer, Jesus the Messiah.*

I live to hear Him speak to me and tell me what He is doing today. I live off every word He says. Jesus has come and spoken to me many times, and I never want Him to stop talking. When I meditate on His Word, the Scriptures, He speaks as though He is standing before me, and He longs to do the same for you. When His words become what we crave the most, He will show up in person or by the Holy Spirit and release the supernatural. Allow the kingdom of God to govern your life, and you will receive your kingdom provisions when you submit to His authority.

Jesus has a unique way of doing things, and we need to allow Him to govern our lives. He wants us to have the kingdom, and He knows what we need in order to participate in it. However, we must never make the mistake of thinking we can ever earn our kingdom rights through pious acts. They are given:

> Do not fear, little flock, for it is your Father's good
> pleasure to give you the kingdom.    Luke 12:32

We think we want His kingdom, but when we realize how much more our heavenly Father wants it for us, it is overwhelming and causes us to humble ourselves before Him. Then He will show Himself strong on our behalf.

Allow yourself to be fully convinced that God has a plan for your life. Frequently meditate on the Word of God and allow it to change your life, and you will reap a harvest.

*The Spirit says, "I have formed you in your mother's womb. You were at one time just a thought and a desire of mine. I put that thought and desire into words, and you became a living soul. I watched you being formed in your mother's womb and wrote a book about you in heaven. Spend all your resources to have My heart and mind and enter into your destiny. Ask that your book be opened and fulfilled every day as you worship and honor Me. I will guide you and teach you, for you are My desire. Enter in!"*

# Chapter 3

# The Divine Pattern

L et's look into the spiritual history of words to better understand my encounter with Jesus and why He would spend time emphasizing the use of words.

There are laws working today that God set in motion at the very beginning of time that are recorded in the book of Genesis. Understanding what is already at work in our world will help us know how to operate on the earth as spiritual beings. We enter into the supernatural realm when we honor and utilize spiritual laws that were created and used by God.

The laws of the natural world govern our physical existence, but some laws can be transcended by more powerful ones. Higher laws supersede lower ones. For example, gravity is a law; however, the laws of lift and thrust can supersede gravity by overcoming it. We enjoy flight because there is a higher law than gravity.

The same rule applies to supernatural laws. We should not deny the natural way of things on earth; however, we should recognize that the Spirit of God and His Word can reveal a higher law, one that supersedes earthly realities.

*When spoken in faith by the Holy Spirit, our words can have the power to change things. Words can take you into your answers, your destiny, by making it possible for the supernatural to overcome things in the natural.*

## BACK TO THE BEGINNING

The book of Hebrews tells us that during creation, all things were created with words:

> By faith we understand that the worlds were framed by the *word* of God, so that the things which are seen were not made of things which are visible.     Hebrews 11:3, emphasis added

Also, we know that it was Jesus, the Son of God, through whom God acted as creator:

> [God] has in these last days spoken to us by *His Son*, whom He has appointed heir of all things, through whom also He *made the worlds*.
> Hebrews 1:2, emphasis added

Let's go back to the book of beginnings, Genesis, to see the actual account:

In the beginning God created the heavens and
the earth. And the earth was without form, and
void; and darkness was upon the face of the
deep. And the Spirit of God moved upon the
face of the waters. And *God said,* Let there be
light: and there was light

> Genesis 1:1–3 KJV, emphasis added

From Genesis 1:3, we learn that "the Spirit of
God was hovering over the face of the waters."
This tells us that the Holy Spirit is ready to
respond to the commands of God spoken
through His Word (Jesus Christ). When God
begins to speak, the heavens stand at attention. In the supernatural sphere, every created
thing is ready to respond to the voice of God.
Notice that after God speaks, whatever He says
immediately happens.

When it came time for Adam to be created, a very powerful detail emerges that explains why Jesus told me that
my words are important. "Then God said, "Let Us *make
man in Our image,* according to Our likeness" (Genesis 1:26,
emphasis added). You have probably heard many times that
God made man in His likeness, but have you considered what
happened to that likeness when Adam sinned? Obviously,
mankind lost some of its likeness to God. We were no longer
sinless or immortal. However, Jesus, through His sacrificial
death, bought us restoration, both spiritually and physically.

The Bible calls Jesus the "second Adam" and tells us that He has gone before us into the Holy of Holies.

In the book of Genesis, we see that God came down to visit with Adam and Eve in the garden (Genesis 3:8–9). God and man had an open, unhindered, and intimate relationship. They were one. Jesus, when conceived by the Holy Spirit, became the second Adam, and He was given the same glory that Adam had before sinning. Because of our relationship with Jesus through the new birth, we are recipients of His glory. In fact, Jesus said, "And the glory which You gave Me I have given them, that they may be one just as We are one" (John 17:22). We share in His glory, but we have to learn how to let it shine through us.

*The Holy Spirit is within us and upon us to lead us into a life of glory. By spending time with God in prayer and the fellowship of His Word, we learn His ways. By meditating on the Word, we eat of heavenly manna and feed our souls, which increases our capacity to shine in a dark world (see John 6:41).*

## MAN: THE SPEAKING SPIRIT

It is amazing that the modern world, despite all its scientific advancements, has so little understanding of mankind, its creator, and the supernatural realm. However, God clearly has given us all that we need through Jesus Christ, including the opportunity to participate in the divine nature. Second Peter 1:4 puts it like this:

By which have been given to us exceedingly great and precious promises, that through these *you may be partakers of the divine nature*, having escaped the corruption that is in the world through lust. (emphasis added)

Also, note these scriptures:

And so it is written, "The first man Adam became a living being." The last Adam [Jesus] became a life-giving spirit.     1 Corinthians 15:45

Have *put on the new man* who is *renewed in knowledge* according to the image of Him who created him.  Colossians 3:10, emphasis added

For though He was crucified in weakness, yet He lives by the power of God. For we also are weak in Him, but *we shall live with Him by the power of God* toward you.
     2 Corinthians 13:4, emphasis added

If then you were raised with Christ, *seek those things which are above*, where Christ is, sitting at the right hand of God. *Set your mind on things above*, not on things on the earth. For you died, and *your life is hidden with Christ* in God.
     Colossians 3:1–3, emphasis added

## ARE YOU BEGGING OR REQUESTING?

Jesus discussed words with me at length during this visitation because He has set up a dominion that operates by certain spiritual laws and principles. It is called the kingdom of God. I have learned that if you follow these principles and respect the kingdom laws, you will not have to plead for spiritual power and blessings. You simply request access to the provisions that have already been made available to you through the name of Jesus.

A study of the word *ask* in the New Testament will reveal that it has a far stronger meaning than we might think. In English, asking is akin to begging. However, the Greek word for *ask* can also be translated as "requiring what is owed." We know that if the God of the universe wants to give us something and has already deposited it into our account, we don't have to ask Him for it again and again or demand things of Him.

*What we must do is place a demand on our heavenly account and make a withdrawal while binding any hindrances in the earth realm, which is under the influence of Satan and his minions. We can command them to stop obstructing what God has purposed for us.*

You see, everything on the earth is not in submission to God as of yet. We must bring correction to that which is not submitted by speaking and demanding evil forces to yield to God's will. Placing a demand causes a release of the kingdom of God into the situation, whatever it might be. Mark 11:23–26 is one of my earthly assignments that I have been charged to teach and live by:

> For assuredly, I say to you, "Whoever says to this mountain, 'Be removed and be cast into the sea,' and does not doubt in his heart, but believes that those things he says will be done, he will have whatever he says. Therefore I say to you, whatever things you ask when you pray, believe that you receive them, and you will have them.
>
> "And whenever you stand praying, if you have anything against anyone, forgive him, that your Father in heaven may also forgive you your trespasses. But if you do not forgive, neither will your Father in heaven forgive your trespasses."
>
> *The fact is, every believer is called to live the life described in these verses. More than you can even imagine is possible for you if you will only believe that the things you say will be done.*

## DEBTS DISCHARGED

I remember when my wife and I started practicing the verses concerning speaking to a mountain. We decided that God wanted us to become debt free, so we started speaking to our debt mountain. From 2000 to 2008, we proclaimed that we were debt free and commanded debt to get out. Soon our debt began to disappear. In 2008, the only debt we had left was our mortgage payment. Obviously, we were careful not to create more debt and did everything we could in the natural to pay off the debt, but we also received supernatural assistance.

At that point, the Lord told me to pay a person's mortgage payment for them. I remember thinking that I would never pay off my own mortgage if I kept handing out money to others to pay theirs. Actually, in a way, I was right. *We didn't pay off our mortgage—God did!* Someone left us enough money in a will to pay off our mortgage in February of 2008.

*Speak to your mountains! God's Word really does perform just as He says it will. God would not have put those verses in the Bible if He did not want us to practice them.*

In Mark 9:23, Jesus said, "If you can believe, all things are possible to him who believes." So what is the problem? Why are we not seeing this truth manifested in our lives as it should be? During this visitation, I realized something about Jesus that I want to share with you on the subject of forgiveness.

## ARE YOU CURSED?

We *must* forgive. Do not allow the enemy to trap you into holding on to offenses. Jesus wants you to be offense free in this life. He has come to make you free (see John 8:36). Hurtful experiences can entangle us in bitterness.

*Jesus wants us to know that the enemy does this to people because he knows that unforgiveness hinders their ability to receive from God.*

God knows we have been wronged, yet He still requires us to forgive. Once we truly forgive, He can answer our prayers. Faith is of the heart, but so is unforgiveness, and it hinders our faith. The enemy will use anything and anyone to disqualify our prayers. We cannot stay hooked into what the Spirit of God is doing if we have offenses that have developed into bitterness. When we are wronged, we cannot reverse the facts or successfully deny them; we can only forgive them.

*Forgiveness unhooks you from a curse so that God can bless you in amazing ways. Don't spend another day allowing offenses to hinder your prayers. If Jesus could forgive while suffering the torment of crucifixion, you can forgive in your situation, too.*

When the disciples could not get their prayers answered, they asked Jesus why. He replied:

> Because of your unbelief; for assuredly, I say to you, if you have faith as a mustard seed, you will say to this mountain, "Move from here to there," and it will move; and nothing will be impossible for you.　　　Matthew 17:20

Words are important, as I found out from Jesus' opening statement during His visitation with me. We can actually curse ourselves with our words:

> If anyone among you thinks he is religious, and does not bridle his tongue but deceives his own heart, this one's religion is useless. James 1:26

> For if we could control our tongues, we would be perfect and could also control ourselves in every other way. . . .

> . . . And among all the parts of the body, the tongue is a flame of fire. It is a whole world of wickedness, corrupting your entire body. It can set your whole life on fire, for it is set on fire by hell itself.

> . . . Sometimes it praises our Lord and Father, and sometimes it curses those who have been

made in the image of God. And so blessing and cursing come pouring out of the same mouth. Surely, my brothers and sisters, this is not right!

James 3:2, 6, 9–10 NLT

You now know the truth, so it is your move. Control your words and forgive, or ignore the truth and continue to be hindered in your prayers.

## HERE'S THE PROOF

I have had several huge financial miracles happen to me as a result of words. Upon graduating from high school, I gave my life to Christ. At that time, I sincerely felt that I wanted to give everything to Him. At a church service shortly after my salvation experience, I wrote a check to the church for every penny I had. I felt that this would express my total commitment to the Lord. I told Him that I would never worry about finances again because He now had all my money.

A year later, I went away to college with only a $100 bill in my pocket that I had received from an elderly woman at a prayer meeting I had attended. That paid for my transportation to college. Now I had to believe for a job at college to pay for my tuition and other needs. Upon arrival, I applied for scholarships and grants, but I still desperately needed a job. I applied to be a dishwasher in the college cafeteria. However, they told me that thirty people had applied before me and that they would be hired ahead of me. I was very disappointed.

After applying, I went to the cafeteria for lunch. While I was eating my meal, the manager of the cafeteria came to my table. He asked if my name was Kevin, and I replied yes. He then told me that if I would go with him and begin washing dishes without delay, he would hire me ahead of the thirty people who preceded me on the list. I left my food on the table, followed him to the work area, and started washing dishes, with a big smile on my face. I had a job!

Later I received grants from the government for some of my expenses. After that, I increased my credit hours per semester. Of course, this also increased my school bill. I was praying about that when I ran into a professor in the phys-ed locker room. I had favor with him because I had beaten the school record in two athletic events. He asked me if I needed anything. I replied that he could believe with me for my college tuition to be paid. He answered, "Oh, that's easy. I don't need to pray about that. I'll take care of it."

The next day, I received a call from the financial office, telling me that I had received another grant. I therefore decided to take classes during the summer as well, so my costs went up again. My bill skyrocketed so much that the university warned me that I would have to sit out a semester or two until the debt was paid.

After receiving that warning, I was at a friend's house, who had a wonderful painting of Jesus on the wall. While pointing at the painting of Jesus, I told Him that I had left everything for Him and knew He wanted to pay off my school bills. It seemed like a lot of money at the time, but I knew He wanted to do it for me. When I spoke those words aloud, I knew they were true and that I was merely voicing the truth. It is not enough to know something is true. You have to speak it out in words because your words release God's will on the earth.

A few weeks after this incident, I got a call from the registrar's office, asking me to visit them. I was well aware that the purpose of this appointment could be to ask me to leave college until I paid my bill. However, when I arrived, the registrar handed me a copy of my school bill with *Paid in Full* written on it. As I sat there listening to the story of how that had happened, it became apparent that Jesus had performed a miracle for me.

The university's financial department was deeply touched by what God had done on my behalf. The registrar told me that a businessman had contacted them, looking for a student with a peculiar last name. God had brought my face before the businessman, as well as my name, during prayer and told him to pay off my school bills. He called all the universities in the city, asking for a student with my last name (which he didn't know how to pronounce), until he finally found my college. The man did not have a clear understanding of why he was doing this; he was simply being obedient to God. The man drove over to my campus and wrote a check for the full amount of my debt, but he requested that I never be told his name.

## YOUR WORDS CAN CHANGE YOUR WORLD

Jesus desires everyone on earth to understand what He has done for them, and it is so much more than many

Christians comprehend. Yes, He saved us from hell and damnation and gave us eternal life, but He also made possible a life of meaning and purpose while we are on the earth. Jesus said it like this in John 10:10: "The robber comes only to steal and to kill and to destroy. I came so they might have life, a great full life" (NLV).

God wants you to begin to take hold of your earthly destiny by beginning to speak the truth about yourself and others. We have been born anew in His image, and we have been given a powerful quickening spirit (1 Corinthians 15:45).

> *Jesus is saying, "Yield to Me, and begin speaking out and prophesying to your world." You can bring correction to your circumstances as you yield and express the truth found in God's Word. Speak it out, and you will see correction come. Everything in all of creation was made by His words, is sustained by His words, and responds to His words (see Psalm 103:20).*

Jesus wants us to participate in the divine nature. As His sons and daughters, we need to find out what is involved in being a son or daughter. Although we want all that God has for us, many of us have found that something we can't identify is holding us back. In the next part of my heavenly encounter, Jesus began showing me things that were keeping me from reaching my maximum potential.

# Chapter 4

# Wounding and Restoring
# of the Soul

꧁꧂

Psalm 23:3 says, "He restores my soul."

Next, Jesus asked me to turn and again look at my body, still in its glorified state as it lay on the operating table. What I saw astounded me. My body had been perfect before, but now a black vest covered the area from my chest to my stomach. I immediately understood that the black area was my soul. The soul is the center of the will and emotions and connects directly to the mind.

Jesus pointed out that my darkened soul was obscuring my beauty, covering my beautiful, glorified body. In a flash, Jesus took me to the table to see the black vest up close. It was made up of the untrue words that had been spoken over me. He explained, "This is a lifetime of words spoken against you, and they continue to affect you." With a wave of His hand, a panoramic view like a large screen appeared, and He began to show me the occasions when those words were spoken.

The pain created by those incidents welled up as I relived them in fast succession. It wasn't long before I began to cry as each incident increased my grief. At this point, Jesus stopped the review. He said, "I did not show you this to upset you, but only to reveal to you that the hurt is still there." He added, "We need to deal with the hurt caused by these words. They are affecting you."

*Each of us has hurtful situations in our past, and even when they are not in our conscious thoughts, they are still affecting us if we have not been healed of them.*

Jesus wanted to show me the contrast between the beauty of my spirit man and my damaged soul. Hurtful words of the past were obscuring who I really was. Many of the people who spoke those damaging things did not understand they were not speaking the truth, my God-ordained destiny. In a sense, without intending to, they were speaking the enemy's intentions over me. I believe everyone has similar hurts that need healing.

*Please take a moment now to allow the Holy Spirit to reveal areas of your life affected by the lies spoken over you. Ask God to begin the healing today.*

## SOUL HEALING

Jesus focused on the effects that words have on our lives, both good and bad. He then revealed to me the four ways that He heals our souls:

1.  Jesus can wave His hand over a person's chest (soul) and heal them immediately.
2.  We can listen to the truth, continually renewing our minds until the lies we have believed about ourselves are replaced with the truth.
3.  We can pray in the Holy Spirit until our inner (spirit) man becomes so powerful that he overthrows the soul with its mind, will, and emotions and becomes the dominant influence.
4.  We can also receive healing through the process of godly counseling.

Each of these has been used successfully in my life and brought me healing.

Let Him have all your hurts. He cares so much about you that Peter, inspired by the Holy Spirit, wrote, "casting all your care upon Him, for He cares for you" (1 Peter 5:7).

Jesus began teaching me about how words bind people. He said, "Don't speak against people, either saved or unsaved. Your words can go out and bind them and hinder My work in their lives." He continued, "Do not even speak against unsaved people, because I am working to bring them to a point of repentance and salvation, and your words can slow down the process." Then He showed me how He was working through angels and humans to bring people into His kingdom and how words help or hinder that activity.

*Do you want to be anointed by the Holy Spirit to take part in God's plans for the unsaved? Do you want to work alongside angels? Then use your words wisely, and allow the Spirit to lead what you say. Doing so will cause you to participate in the supernatural.*

## PRAYING IN THE SPIRIT

During that 1992 visitation, Jesus spent much of the time discussing the Holy Spirit's operation in the believer's life. He discussed praying in the Spirit as if it were necessary for everyone, not optional. Clearly, He considered it to be important for His disciples of today. Jesus encouraged me to pray often in the Spirit and emphasized that it is the single most important activity for walking in the supernatural.

*As Jesus urged me, I encourage you to make praying in the Spirit a part of your life every day.*

Study the following passage of Scripture to better understand how the Holy Spirit wants to operate in your life. In 1 Corinthians 2:4–5, 9–16, Paul said:

And my speech and my preaching were not with persuasive words of human wisdom, but in *demonstration of the Spirit* and of power, that your faith should not be in the wisdom of men but in the power of God....

But as it is written: "Eye has not seen, nor ear heard, nor have entered into the heart of man the things which God has prepared for those who love Him." But God has *revealed them to us through His Spirit.* For *the Spirit searches all things*, yes, the deep things of God. For what man knows the things of a man except the spirit of the man which is in him? Even so *no one knows the things of God except the Spirit of God.* Now we have received, not the spirit of the world, but *the Spirit who is from God, that we might know the things that have been freely given to us* by God.

These things we also speak, not in words which man's wisdom teaches but which *the Holy Spirit teaches*, comparing spiritual things with spiritual. But the natural man does not receive *the things of the Spirit of God*, for they are foolishness to him; nor can he know them, because they *are spiritually discerned.* But *he who is spiritual judges all things*, yet he himself is rightly judged by no one. For "who has known the mind of the Lord that he may instruct Him?" (emphasis added)

By praying in the Spirit, we yield to a process through which God communicates His heart to us.

*Jesus wants us to know that prayer in the Spirit can bring the actual heart of God into us and make it possible for us to express those wonderful truths in the physical realm.*

## SPIRIT POWER

During this hour-long heavenly encounter with Jesus, He made me aware of what yielding to the Spirit of God can accomplish. I learned that we can receive wisdom by spending time praying in the Spirit. According to Acts 1:8, mankind received the Spirit of God on the day of Pentecost to empower us to live supernaturally and enable us to testify effectively of Him. Supernatural ability is available to us from the Holy Spirit. God wants to help us, and this is a way that He can do it.

The Bible says the same power that raised Jesus from the dead dwells in you (Romans 8:11). Think about that for a minute. You have supernatural power within you because the Spirit of God lives in you. The Holy Spirit can help you be a victor in any situation. I learned that He does not plan for you to ever live a defeated life. Rather, He has a step-by-step plan for every predicament you will ever face to make it turn out for your good. Never doubt this: He loves you and wants the best for you.

Next, Jesus began speaking to me about my millionaire friend who would be picking me up after the operation. He said, "You tell _____ that if he will pray in My Spirit more often, I will help him with his finances and keep him out of legal trouble." He continued, "This is the amount he will be worth at the end of his life *without* My help," and the big screen where I had watched the hurtful events from my past displayed a very large number: $32 million. Then Jesus continued, "But if he will yield to My spirit and pray, he will be worth this amount at the end of His life." The amount now revealed on the screen was approximately four times the first amount, almost $140 million. It was humbling to realize that the Holy Spirit wants to help people prosper in *every* area of life.

## THINGS TO COME

To illustrate the Holy Spirit's desire to tell us future events, I want to tell you about what happened to me concerning 9/11.

On September 7, 2001, I was loading my car to go visit friends in the mountains outside Phoenix, Arizona, when I sensed someone walk up behind me. The presence of God became so strong that I felt weak and bowed my head without turning. Then I heard a voice say, "The worst incident in aviation history will happen next week. There is coming a time when America will be recovering from one incident when another immediately takes place. The incidents will increase in frequency until they come one after another." In a moment, I saw many types of devastating events, not just aviation disasters. My first thought was, "I'm flying next week!" (I work for a major airline as a flight attendant.)

On Friday, September 7, the Holy Spirit told me to change my schedule to a flight leaving late Tuesday morning on September 11. I watched the entire September 11 attack on television at the airport office. Soon they told me to go home and canceled my flights for the next four days. Had I flown my original schedule, I would have been in New York on September 11, but God's visitation protected me from harm.

The visit with Jesus in the operating room reminded me that the Holy Spirit reveals the future (see John 16:13). God actually has a plan for you written down in heaven. The psalmist revealed it in Psalm 139:16: "You saw me before I was born. Every day of my life was recorded in your book. Every moment was laid out before a single day had passed" (NLT).

*Every person on earth has a book written about them in heaven. God created every person with a plan and purpose in mind. He wrote about each day of your life long ago in a book with your name on it located on a bookshelf in heaven.*

God gave us the Holy Spirit to help us know two books: the Word of God and the book of our life's story. Because heaven resides outside of time, your future is now. God does not intend for you to be devastated or to fail (see Jeremiah

29:11). Jesus, the captain of your salvation, has already won a mighty victory for you and your destiny. He came to give you an exceedingly abundant life (see John 10:10). You don't have to allow the thief to destroy your destiny.

God has assigned the wonderful person called the Holy Spirit to teach you how to walk successfully through this life and to tell you of things to come. We need to learn to live the life we were designed for. Because He is the Spirit of truth, He will lead us along our true path. Make this promise from Jesus your reality:

> But the Helper, the Holy Spirit, whom the Father will send in My name, He will teach you all things, and bring to your remembrance all things that I said to you. John 14:26

As we begin to yield to the Holy Spirit and let go of our own ways, He will teach us to understand His ways. He will make it possible for us to experience everything written about us in our heavenly biographies.

Jesus taught me that day about making ourselves available for His purposes and allowing heaven to be formed in us by praying in the Spirit.

*There will be a divine explosion in your heart as God makes the truths in this chapter real to you. Yield to the Spirit and to God's Word, and decide to arise to your destiny.*

# Chapter 5

# The Weapons of Your Warfare

Next, Jesus announced that He was going to show me the effectiveness of our prayers. He extended His arm and pointed.

## PRAYERS PRODUCE SHOCK WAVES

Instantly, as though the destination had come to us, we were standing on a mountaintop overlooking what appeared to be White Sands Missile Range in New Mexico. As we stood there, He said to me, "Here is what happens when you begin to pray." Then a fireball resembling an atomic explosion erupted. As we watched, the plume created by the fireball towered high above us. Jesus then pointed out a shock wave that was traveling away from the explosion in every direction. The shock wave came quickly and with great intensity, and it was so powerful that it removed everything standing in its path.

After this illustration of how powerful our prayers are, Jesus encouraged me to never give up on my prayers and to always pray with intensity and faith. Even when I did not see changes or immediate results, He told me to continue praying and see it through to the end. He said, "You see, your prayers *are* effective; they *do* work."

From this revelation, I realized that when we pray, a shock wave emanates from us that levels everything in its path. Anything hindering the answer, it pushes out of the way. I understood that nothing is impossible to you or me when we believe, and that all things actually are possible through Him (see Mark 9:23). Please never underestimate the massive power released by the Holy Spirit to answer your prayers.

> *He taught me that we are to be infused with the breath of heaven, speaking God's words for God's purposes on the earth about those things that concern us. By speaking with God's authority, we allow Him to advance His kingdom through us and for us.*

## TRANSLATION DURING INTERCESSION

Although I have many unusual prayer stories, I chose the following one to show you that God wants you to take the limits off your prayer life. This story involves being translated.

In my last year of college, my schedule included a time of prayer in the morning from about three until six. I had finished my bachelor's degree a year early (in three years) but remained in school to get a double major. In previous years, I had worked during the school year; but during my fourth year, I did not work but instead studied a great deal. I found that I was unable to keep pace with God's work in my life without those three hours of morning prayer.

One morning as I prayed, I felt a divine urgency to intercede for a friend who was having financial problems. She had told me that she might have to take time off from her education until she could pay her school bill. As I fervently prayed for her in the Spirit with my eyes closed, I remembered the time when I had found myself in the same predicament.

Then suddenly I felt like I was flying, and air seemed to blow past me. I still did not open my eyes, but suddenly I sensed that I was in a different place from the chapel where I had been praying. The ambience, the temperature, and the odors were different. Then I felt compelled to speak boldly to my friend, as if she were directly in front of me.

I declared to her what God had revealed to me. With my eyes still closed, I told her that she was not leaving college because she was called to be there. Then I seemed to immediately leave that room and return to my dorm's prayer chapel. Not understanding what had happened, I thought no more about the event.

Months later, as we were getting ready to graduate, we were walking together and talking because she had typed my college thesis. I told her how thankful I was for her help and how glad I was that she had remained in school that year. During our conversation, she mentioned that about a year ago, she had recorded in her journal a night when she awakened to find me standing at the foot of her bed, loudly praying and prophesying to her. I was so loud that she feared I would awaken her roommates.

During my visit, she kept telling me to quiet down, but I continued loudly proclaiming God's will over her while standing at the foot of the bed. When I stopped talking, I suddenly disappeared. At the time, she could not understand how I had gotten through so many locked security doors to reach her room. In addition, our dorms were distant from each other. I studied the dates and times with her and discovered a match with the time I had prayed for her in my dorm chapel and felt like I was whisked to another room.

## YOU *CAN* MAKE A DIFFERENCE

Jesus began to explain to me the incredible difference a person can make on earth when they live in their authority as a son or daughter of God.

*The revelation of God's Word you walk in directly affects the scope of your spirit man's authority and influence in the kingdom.*

He said, "For example, your area of authority extends thirty feet around you. You have developed your spirit to have authority in that geographic area. People within that perimeter will be under your spiritual influence and will encounter the power and authority you walk in." He continued, "I have men on the earth who affect whole cities with their presence when they enter them." These men had developed their spirit man to affect an area that size. Jesus then showed me an apostle I knew. As I watched him enter a city, every devil knew he was there. When he spoke, the city responded because of his sphere of authority.

Jesus taught me how to extend my area of influence by attending to my spiritual life. This is accomplished by feeding your heart with God's truth and living uprightly before Him. We have to prepare our natural environment to support our spiritual growth. I had to eliminate some things from my life and add other things to reach the desired result. Things that are okay for others to do may not be okay for you. You have to let the Holy Spirit and God's Word guide you into what things are best for you. Some people in your life may have to go, and others may need to enter it. This is all part of the process of increasing your power and authority so you can fulfill your mission on earth.

*God is helping to create the right environment for you to grow and function correctly in His perfect will for you. However, you have to do your part, too.*

After my visit with Jesus, I began to see my circle of authority operate more powerfully. Your authority is with you all the time, and if you look for it, you can see it revealed daily in your life. Let me give you an example.

Remember, I work for a major airline as a flight attendant. One afternoon I was on a long flight. I had finished my service in the front of the airplane when I noticed people beginning to gather in the front. I came out of the galley to investigate why people were congregating. This airplane had six seat lounges facing each other at the front of the aircraft. A woman who claimed to have psychic powers (a witch) had agreed to do readings for people by inquiring of spirits through the use of tarot cards.

That was a mistake on her part, since I forbid the trafficking of familiar spirits in my realm of authority. Leviticus 19:31 warns, "Regard not them that have familiar spirits, neither seek after wizards, to be defiled by them: I am the Lord your God" (KJV). As I watched, people were eagerly coming forward to hear what the devil had to say.

I couldn't believe this was happening on an airplane with people that God had assigned me to look after. Even the flight attendant from the back of the plane was lined up to hear what the devil might say to her. She expressed her eagerness to me, and then I broke *my* exciting news to her. I told her it would not work because I was going to stop it by praying silently in the Spirit. I declared in Jesus' name that the evil spirits would not be able to manifest. She did not believe me and thought there was nothing evil about it.

The witch began the reading for the first victim and laid down the cards. As words were about to come from her mouth, she stopped. She turned and told everyone that there was interference, and she could not do the readings at this time. She picked up her cards, put them away, and all the disappointed inquirers returned to their seats. The flight attendant who had not believed that I could stop the readings looked at me, shocked. I told her that what I had was greater than the devil, and today she is a believer.

> *You also have authority over the devil in the name of Jesus. You never have to allow him or those who do his work to act within your area of authority.*

# Chapter 6

# Matters of Death and Life, Hell and Heaven

Jesus shared with me about the time He spent in hell after dying on the cross. He said during the time He was cut off from the Father and the Holy Spirit, He experienced torment and punishment for everyone's sins so that we could escape the pain and punishment we deserve. No human being needs to go to hell because Jesus paid the debt created by all our sins.

He was extremely passionate when He talked about His anguish of separation from God. He said that He had to go deep within Himself to remember and rehearse His identity with the Father because circumstances were screaming the opposite.

## ABANDONED BY GOD

Think about it: Jesus had never experienced a moment without the Father's presence until He was dying on the cross and uttered, "'Eli, Eli, lama sabachthani?' that is, 'My God, My God, why have You forsaken Me?'" (Matthew 27:46). Satan thought he had defeated Jesus until He received the command from the Father to walk out of hell and take with Him the righteous dead. The apostle Paul reported in the book of Ephesians, "When He ascended on high, He led captivity captive, and gave gifts to men" (Ephesians 4:8–9). In Revelation 1:18, Jesus says of Himself, "I am He who lives, and was dead, and behold, I am alive forevermore. Amen. And I have the keys of Hades and of Death."

The Father promised Jesus that by His following through with the salvation plan, God would unite humanity with Him in a plan for their redemption. Jesus expressed to me with great emotion, in a broken voice, the anguish He went through for us and His great longing that I share its importance with everyone who would listen:

> And being found in appearance as a man, He humbled Himself and became obedient to the point of death, even the death of the cross. Therefore God also has highly exalted Him and given Him the name which is above every name, that at the name of Jesus every knee should bow, of those in heaven, and of those on earth, and of those under the earth, and that every tongue should confess that Jesus Christ is Lord, to the glory of God the Father.       Philippians 2:8–11

Throughout His short life on earth, Jesus allowed the Holy Spirit to reveal the scriptures that mentioned His life as the Messiah. From those words, while still a boy He gained insight into experiences that were to come. Thus the Bible says that Jesus increased in wisdom, stature, and favor (see Luke 2:52).

The writings of David and others about the Messiah were a necessary part of Jesus' education. The following prophetic passage was a source of comfort and guidance to Jesus during His time in hell:

> I have set the LORD always before me; because He is at my right hand I shall not be moved. Therefore my heart is glad, and my glory rejoices; my flesh also will rest in hope. For *You will not leave my soul in Sheol, nor will You allow Your Holy One to see corruption.* You will show me the path of life; in Your presence is fullness of joy; at Your right hand are pleasures forevermore.          Psalm 16:8–11, emphasis added

## PASSION IS PERTINENT TO PERFORMANCE

As Jesus was sharing this intense time of His life, the Holy Spirit expanded my understanding about what Jesus was teaching me. Everything He says has multiple levels of meaning, and He gives new layers of understanding each time we allow Him to speak to us. I came to understand that He was giving me insight into living a victorious life.

It is vitally important that I help you understand something that was of utmost importance to Him:

*As a person who lived in a human body, Jesus is familiar with our weaknesses. Yes, He even has kindheartedness toward us when we blow it! Hebrews 4:15 makes this clear: "For we do not have a High Priest who cannot sympathize with our weaknesses, but was in all points tempted as we are, yet without sin."*

Jesus also explained why hell is such a terrible place. The demons of hell continually challenge and torment those there about their weaknesses and failures. They constantly mock, devalue, make fun of, and remind them of mistakes. It quickly becomes unbearable but continues throughout eternity. Hell was made for the devil and his angels (Matthew 25:41)—*not* for man.

The enemy jeered Jesus for His supposed failure to succeed in His mission to bring God's kingdom to earth. He was ridiculed for not being the actual Son of God as He claimed. He was dishonored because the Father had abandoned Him, and He was belittled for His stupidity in not bowing down and worshiping Satan during His temptation in the desert (see Matthew 4:9). And they did it over and over.

*Jesus wants every person to understand that during our earthly lives, we will have trouble, but He has overcome the world (see John 16:33). The overcoming power Jesus used to escape from the depths of hell was placed inside you when you were born of the Spirit of God. You merely need to yield to what Jesus attained for you (see Philippians 3:12). The victory is already inside you, and you can release it by His Spirit. Make no mistake—demon spirits will try to discourage and hinder you, just as they did Jesus during the time He spent in hell; but like Him, you have the power to overcome every adversity and circumstance that stands between you and being raised to victory.*

The torments of hell can happen to you on earth. It may seem that something strange is happening to you (1 Peter 4:12), but it might be a fiery trial from hell. Jesus sent me back to tell you that you must confront demonic spirits with heaven's truth, as He did. It will require conviction and intensity on your part. The Bible calls this *zeal*.

However, no fervor means no overcoming the encounter with your enemy. You must *enforce* your victory over the enemy. If you don't, not only will he stay, but he will also take more ground in your life. You must live with God's purpose as the center of your life and become a warrior who imposes God's purpose with intensity. You must develop a conviction that God's purpose for your life will withstand any onslaught and that it is more powerful than any of the enemy's plans.

## PASSIONATE PRAYER

Another understanding I received about Jesus' time in hell had to do with the importance of intensity in prayer. Because of Jesus' trials before He preached to the spirits in prison and rose from the dead, He has something to teach us about reaching deep within ourselves to overcome any adversity.

> *Although we can't comprehend what Jesus went through for us, we can learn from His fierceness in opposing Satan. We can emulate His steadfastness and endurance in our prayers and declarations during difficult times. In James 5:16, the Bible tells us what kind of prayer works: "The effective, fervent prayer of a righteous man avails much."*

Let me give you an example of intensity in prayer during a life-or-death situation to communicate the necessity of living your spiritual life on a more passionate level. While making a solo training flight for my commercial pilot's license from Phoenix to Nogales, Arizona, near the Mexican border, the worst thing possible happened. However, everything had looked good during my preflight checks, so I took off and climbed to my cruising altitude. As air traffic control (ATC) handed me off to Tucson ATC, I noticed a couple of problems with the airplane. Had I been flying with a copilot, I would have been able to look into them and land in Tucson. During my quick inspection, they did not appear to be major, so I continued on without realizing the airplane was developing more serious problems.

When I became aware that I had a systems failure, I turned back toward Tucson, but because of instrument failure, I did not realize that I had drifted far south of my course. I entered a holding pattern and checked my fuel and other gauges, but because of strong winds, I was pushed further off course to the south. Next, I realized that my gas gauges had also failed, and the fuel tanks were almost empty. I called air traffic control for assistance and asked them to locate me on radar. They discovered that I was south of the Mexican border, and I knew that I did not have enough fuel to reach the United States.

It was mountainous below me, and no airports were within reach. I climbed to a higher altitude for a better view and longer glide path and began praying. I sensed the spirit of death come and begin to fasten itself on me, but I prayed with passion from the depths of my spirit and broke through.

Looking down again, I now could see a mine ahead with a dirt road leading to it, and the Lord said, "Land on it." I set up the aircraft for landing and put the plane down on the dirt road. When I came to a stop, unfriendly-looking gang members were shouting threateningly in Spanish as they surrounded my aircraft.

Then I noticed an SUV coming rapidly down the road toward me. The driver turned out to be a high-ranking Mexican official with connections to the FBI. When air traffic control discovered that I was over the border, they must have contacted the FBI, who must have asked this official to try a rescue. His presence held the cartel members at bay. He told me later that when he drove up, they were talking about killing me and taking the airplane. My fervent prayers spared me that day.

We checked the airplane's tanks and discovered they were both empty. He helped me get fuel and despite the mechanical problems, I took off and returned to the United States unharmed, with a new passion to live with greater intensity and pray into the supernatural every day. God truly is our high tower and fortress, as Psalm 144:2 tells us.

## IT'S LATER THAN YOU THINK

Next, Jesus began discussing with me the times in which we live and our closeness to the end of the age. He spoke of men whom He had called and trained for important missions. One man He discussed at length was Moses, the man born with the purpose of delivering the Hebrews from their Egyptian oppressors. Satan tried to kill him as a baby, but God preserved him, and he grew up in Pharaoh's household, where he was destined to become the next pharaoh.

You probably know this story. When Moses was about forty years old, he saw an Egyptian mistreating one of his people, the Hebrews, and killed the Egyptian. He then had to flee into the Midian desert, where he spent another forty years. When Moses encountered the burning bush and was called to deliver God's people from their oppressors, he had been in training for eighty years. While living in Pharaoh's household, he learned how to negotiate with Pharaoh as an ambassador from God for the Hebrews' release. As a sheep-herder in the Sinai for forty years, he learned how to shep-herd the people through the desert to the Promised Land.

In reference to Moses' eighty years of training, Jesus said to me with great seriousness, "I used to have years to get My people ready for what I called them to do, but now I have only days in comparison." He continued, "The time is short," and He explained that we need to be faithful, understand the time in which we live, and allow God to complete our preparation for the coming season.

*Each of us has a role to play in the end-time scenario. We are to humble ourselves, seek the Lord to understand our purpose, and then do our job passionately. The Lord is sending help from His throne to get us ready.*

## HELP IS ON THE WAY

As an example of the help God is sending, take hope from a supernatural intervention I had in college. Because of this encounter, I was kept from harm and delay in my prepara-tion for service. God sent a mighty angel to help me, and He will help you, too.

When I attended school, I was very excited to be there. Everything was new, and I wanted to get the most out of my time there. I was on a partial scholarship, so I had to keep my grade point average up to remain qualified for it. I needed to study most of the time because I was not then a person who learned easily and quickly.

The university had frequent social functions, and everything seemed inviting, but I did not have enough time to do everything I wanted. I was meeting many new people, who frequently asked me to attend these events. I wondered how they could get their studies done when they were always out having fun. Finally, I felt that these activities were competing with my spiritual life, and the Lord started reminding me why He had sent me to college. It was difficult, but I became more disciplined and stayed in my room studying instead of socializing. I had to shut my drapes to eliminate the distraction of the activities outside my room.

As the weeks and months went by, I began spending more time in prayer. I felt that I had been warned by the Holy Spirit that I would miss what the Lord had for me if I did not use my time wisely. As my prayer time increased, so did my hunger for God, and I noticed that my sensitivity to the spirit realm had become greater. I started missing meals (fasting) and spending that time in prayer as I became hungrier for Him than for food. Then one night I had a mighty visitor.

While pacing the floor of my room and praying, the door (which I had shut and locked) flew open. In the doorway stood a large, imposing-looking being who was dressed in full Roman-soldier-type armor; he was eight to nine feet tall. The minute he stepped inside my room, a powerful presence swept over me, and I collapsed to the floor as if I had fainted. I couldn't move and felt overwhelmed and paralyzed. This mighty warrior walked up to me, knelt down, and touched me with his hand. Then I was immediately strengthened, and he helped me to my feet. He was magnificent, and when I looked into his eyes, I saw his complete lack of fear.

Towering over me and speaking in a bold, precise manner, he announced, "I have been sent from Almighty God to give you this message: do not associate with this group of people." In a flash, I saw about fifteen people from school who had recently befriended me. "They are about to be exposed, and God doesn't want you to have anything to do with them." That shocked me because I did not think there was anything wrong with them.

He continued talking but then stopped in the middle of a sentence. He was obviously listening to someone I could not hear or see. When he finished listening, he did not finish his message to me. Instead, he said, "I have to go. I am called to another place. Go down the hall right now [to the prayer room], and the Holy Spirit will finish this message."

In my youthful ignorance, I made a mistake. I told this mighty warrior that he should finish the message, since he was here. Ignoring me, he turned, stepped into the hallway, pointed down the hall, and ordered, "I said go—now!" Then he quickly walked away in the opposite direction. I could sense that he was not pleased with me as he left. He was unlike other angels I had encountered; he seemed to be a warrior.

I did go to the prayer room, where the Holy Spirit confirmed and reiterated what the warrior angel had spoken and then gave me more details about why that group of people would be expelled.

The Holy Spirit told me that I was to continue to listen to my heart, which was telling me to stay separated to myself for a period of time. He confirmed that I was being protected and that this was a vulnerable time for me. There are times when God will have you focus solely on your assignment and ask you to spend quality time with Him rather than engage in other pursuits. The Holy Spirit confirmed my destiny that day in the prayer room and encouraged me to remain faithful.

Six months after that visitation, the college expelled each individual in that group, and they were never seen again. I was grateful that God had sent a messenger to keep me from making a mistake that could have delayed or derailed preparation for my destiny.

*Since God is serious about watching over your destiny and even protects your future with heavenly beings (whether or not you notice them), it is time for you also to get serious. This is the season to find your passion and intensely pursue God and His purpose for your life. During this end-time season, heaven, hell, life, and death are at stake for billions of people, and you have a unique role to play in the end-time drama.*

# Chapter 7

# Wishing and Waffling, or Faith and Faithfulness

L et's explore another subject that Jesus spoke about to me. He told me that I was slated to die and be with Him that day, that I had finished my race.

Wait a minute. I thought that I had to live a long life to finish my race. I wanted to understand because it differed from what I had been taught. When the Spirit of truth visits, we discover that not everything we believe is accurate. Our false ideas need correcting by the whole counsel of God—His Word. There are many witnesses testifying to the truth, if we pay attention. When we have ears to hear, our understanding will be enlightened.

Heaven's government has many ways to confirm what God has said and is saying. Even angels, His holy agents, are "ministering spirits sent to those who are going to inherit salvation" (Hebrews 1:14). They are part of God's government called the "kingdom of God," and they testify and enforce what God is saying. It is not how long we live, but how faithful we are with what is given to us.

Smiling, Jesus continued, "You have done everything I ever asked you to do. You have been faithful." I thought, "I am only thirty-one years old and have accomplished nothing that I hoped to." I had only obeyed my inner man, the voice of my heart, as God led me on my journey. I stood at the end of my life on earth beside my body in an operating room, with Jesus telling me, "You are faithful." That was a moment I will always remember. Although I had not lived a full length of life, I had been faithful with the time that was given to me.

## FORMIDABLE WAY OF LIFE

Looking over my life, I recalled giving up several things I had wanted to do in order to follow God's will for my life. I had discarded positions of honor in the world's estimation, and many times it wasn't easy. There were moments I had felt like I was going backwards, which I discovered is common among people following Jesus.

*The Holy Spirit will lead you in various directions to free you from the world's system. At the time, it may seem unpleasant and even illogical, but you cannot live according to human understanding, this world's wisdom, or the spirit behind it. Allow God to release you from deception and make you free to follow Him.*

Proverbs 3:5 says, "Trust in the Lord with all your heart, and lean not on your own understanding." When Jesus walked the earth, He often challenged those who came to Him to do something illogical in order to follow Him or receive their miracle. You take part in your miracle as you yield to the Spirit of God. Ask the Lord daily to give you a fresh revelation from His realm. The revelation of divine truth will create a change in your reality, and it's time for a reality check from heaven.

Jesus said in John 16:13–15:

> However, when He, the Spirit of truth, has come, He will guide you into *all truth*; for He will not speak on His own authority, but whatever He hears He will speak; and He will tell you things to come. He will glorify Me, for He will take of what is Mine and declare it to you. All things that the Father has are Mine. Therefore I said that He will take of Mine and declare it to you. (emphasis added)

You might be surprised when the Spirit of truth begins separating you from the world system. God has already ordained your separation from the world and commanded it, but we are sometimes slow or resistant and need encouragement. The process of disconnecting from the things of the world and connecting with the things of God is called sanctification. It is little understood by most Christians, infrequently mentioned, and when taught, it is often misunderstood to be a list of things not to do.

Some groups have sequestered themselves and are examples of those who misunderstood sanctification and made it an outward thing only rather than a circumcision of the heart as well. However, sanctification, separation from the world's way of doing and thinking, is absolutely necessary for living the supernatural lifestyle. Second Corinthians 6:17–7:1 teaches:

> "*Come out* from among them and *be separate*," says the Lord. "Do not touch what is unclean, and I will receive you. I will be a Father to you, and you shall be My sons and daughters," says the Lord Almighty. Therefore, having these promises, beloved, let us cleanse ourselves from all filthiness of the flesh and spirit, perfecting holiness in the fear of God. (emphasis added)

When God is allowed to bring you out of the beliefs and practices of this fallen world, His power can manifest to and through you.

*The supernatural realm is waiting for you to be set apart from the worldly realm. Let's prepare ourselves and enter the supernatural realm without delay.*

## GOD'S INVESTMENT PLAN

What Jesus said still resounds within me as if spoken today: "You are faithful."

> *The lesson was that it was not the* quantity *of my life during my thirty-one years on earth that Jesus lauded; it was the* quality *and* obedience *of my life. Whatever God gives you—whether talents, insight, wisdom, or opportunities—is what you are responsible for. He is looking for an increase in His kingdom because of your gifts and your obedience. God's plan for your success is to invest in you and then reward you for following His ways and achieving results.*

If that sounds familiar, you might be recalling Jesus' parable of the talents in Matthew 25:14–30:

> For the kingdom of heaven is like a man traveling to a far country, who called his own servants and delivered his goods to them. And to one he gave five talents, to another two, and to another one, to each according to his own ability; and immediately he went on a journey. Then he who had received the five talents went and traded with them, and made another five talents. And likewise he who had received two gained two more also. But he who had received

one went and dug in the ground, and hid his lord's money. After a long time the lord of those servants came and settled accounts with them.

So he who had received five talents came and brought five other talents, saying, "Lord, you delivered to me five talents; look, I have gained five more talents besides them." His lord said to him, "Well done, good and faithful servant; *you were faithful over a few things, I will make you ruler over many things.* Enter into the joy of your lord." He also who had received two talents came and said, "Lord, you delivered to me two talents; look, I have gained two more talents besides them." His lord said to him, "Well done, good and faithful servant; you have been faithful over a few things, I will make you ruler over many things. Enter into the joy of your lord." (emphasis added)

You probably remember the servant who received one talent and buried it; he was condemned by his lord, called unfaithful, and punished.

*This is hard to hear, but should we fail to use our gifts to build God's kingdom on earth after receiving His greatest gift, salvation, we too will be accountable for squandering what we were given.*

## BLUE ANGEL PERFORMANCE

In Sacramento, California, several years ago, I was between flights when I had a powerful angelic visitation. Having just returned from a nearby shopping mall, I was settling into my hotel room when the atmosphere began shifting. At first, it was very still and peaceful, and then a blue glow began to appear. The presence of God was so powerful that I had to sit down.

Two angels then came into my room, walking through a closed door, and began speaking to me about God's plan for my life. They began to explain why I had gone through so much hardship in my life. The Lord, through them, explained how He had allowed these very difficult situations to develop my character. As I learned to stand up under the challenges, I was enabled to walk with the Lord in a unique and special way. They explained that the magnitude of what I had experienced increased my capacity to trust and walk with the Lord by faith through places where few were called to go.

The angels told me to call my wife in Phoenix and keep her on the line as they talked to me. I called and told her what was happening in my room and began repeating word for word the angels' communications to me. After a few minutes, my wife, who was almost eight hundred miles away, began experiencing a display of God's presence similar to mine. She could sense God's presence through the phone, and we enjoyed this angelic encounter alongside each other.

I learned that the Lord trusted me and wanted me to understand that the intense warfare I had experienced was training for what was to come. The tests and trials were fierce, but now I live in a place where I often see miracles every day.

*God knows the preparation you need for the future He has planned for you. Allow God to work His plan in your life. The enemy cannot win against you because God's hand is on you. His plans will become known at the proper time.*

The angels explained that preparation is constantly going on behind the scenes in order to prepare us to fulfill our destinies on the earth. The enemy attempts to hinder us from reaching our destinies when we are prepared and properly educated in the things of God. The angels finished their message to us and walked out of the room. The powerful presence of God lingered in both our rooms for a time.

## THE SECRET TO POWER: WEAKNESS

I shared the preceding experience because God wants you to know that *your* life counts. Don't wait another day to seek God and learn His ways so that you can get on track for your life's purpose. Allow the hand of God to touch you. In the name of Jesus, I command your enemies to scatter! I believe the Spirit of God has a word for you now:

*"If you will yield to Me and give yourself to Me, I will take you to places you have never thought possible.*

*Where I'm taking you can be accessed only by following My Spirit; allow Me to prepare you for what is to come. I will give you access to the spirit realm as you yield your spirit, soul, and body to me. Don't allow your heart to be troubled; impossible situations prepare you for the supernatural. My power is surely made manifest through your weakness."*

You are in much the same place as Moses was when God spoke to him through the burning bush about delivering His people. Moses faced impossible situations, which God used to propel him into the supernatural. As you read the following, consider if you might have felt the same way Moses did when God asked him to do the impossible. Then notice that God elevated the mission to a higher level, the supernatural realm, and then gifted Moses with supernatural abilities:

Then Moses answered and said, "But suppose they will not believe me or listen to my voice; suppose they say, 'The LORD has not appeared to you.'"

So the LORD said to him, "What is that in your hand?"                    He said, "A rod."

And He said, "Cast it on the ground." So he cast it on the ground, and it became a serpent; and Moses fled from it. Then the LORD said to Moses, "Reach out your hand and take it by the tail" (and he reached out his hand and caught it, and it became a rod in his hand), "that they may believe that the Lord God of their fathers, the God of Abraham, the God of Isaac, and the God of Jacob, has appeared to you."     Exodus 4:1–5

*When you find yourself in a position of weakness, the power of God makes it into a strength. Why does God do it that way? It is because He cannot use people who depend on their own abilities. You qualify for His power only when you are in a place of weakness and humility, out of alternatives yet trusting in Him.*

The Spirit and the Word will work in you until the day comes that you can declare with the apostle Paul:

I have been crucified with Christ; it is no longer I who live, but Christ lives in me; and *the life which I now live in the flesh I live by faith* in the Son of God, who loved me and gave Himself for me.
> Galatians 2:20, emphasis added

And He said to me, "My grace is sufficient for you, for *My strength is made perfect in [your] weakness.*" Therefore most gladly I will rather boast in my infirmities, *that the power of Christ may rest upon me.*
> 2 Corinthians 12:9, emphasis added

When you understand and submit to this work of God in your life, your weaknesses become a divine setup for supernatural intervention. Learn that it is time to yield to the supernatural whenever you sense your weakness and inability to face what stands before you. This requires faith, but you can do this, because despite your feelings, "God has dealt to each one a measure of faith" (Romans 12:3).

The Holy Spirit is with you, and He does not know defeat. Impossible situations reveal your weakness and cause you to trust in God to move you toward your miracle. The supernatural realm is where God lives, and He is calling you to step into it. The Spirit says:

> *"This is your appointed time to step through the door of provision. Do not look at your need, but see Him who is invisible and know that I have your answer in My hand. I am willing, the Spirit is willing, but the flesh is weak. Yield to the Spirit and receive so that your joy may be full."*

## LIVING BEYOND THE NATURAL

My occupation requires me to be out of town much of the time, and I've had this position for twenty-seven years. I have been tested by alarming situations, both mentally and physically. The enemy has attacked me, but my Father has taken care of me by sending His angels to protect me.

You will face situations that are unfamiliar and contrary to your wishes. However, because you know what God's

Word says about His will for you, you will see His desires for you carried out. Because of my visitations with Jesus and His angels, I have learned to depend on what God, His Word, and His kingdom are saying and doing instead of on my earthly circumstances. You are to become what God has already said about you.

Several years ago, I learned to start my day by praying, "If You do not go with me today, Lord, I will fail. Without You, I am nothing. But with You, I will succeed." I depend on Him with a sense of urgency. I have had to overcome sickness and fear until they finally bowed to the mighty power of God and I found relief.

The Holy Spirit's assignment is to lead us into all truth. *Truth* can be translated as "reality." We could all use a dose of heavenly reality. You see, He is with you. Just acknowledge Him daily, and He will lead you into all truth.

*I ask God to give you His reality, a heavenly atmosphere around you that soaks you and causes revelation of His Word to explode within you. I declare it in the name of Jesus!*

The Lord may put you in situations that are beyond your skills and talents, but He will never place you in circumstances beyond your ability as a spirit being. God is waiting for you to invite the Holy Spirit into your circumstances. He will reveal His wishes, provide wisdom, and apply the power and ability necessary to carry out His desire in your circumstances.

You may need to spend time in the presence of the Lord, meditating on His Word and praying in the Spirit, to get the spiritual reality that belongs to you. By doing these things, you will become mature and learn to respond to God's voice more quickly.

*The goal is to become firmly convinced of whom we believe in and what we believe. This will allow us to see who we are in Him.*

## ARE YOU PERSUADED, REALLY?

As you read the following scripture, look for keys to living a life beyond your present limits, a supernatural life:

That Christ may dwell in your hearts through faith; that you, being rooted and grounded in love, may be able to comprehend with all the saints what is the width and length and depth and height—to know the love of Christ which passes knowledge; *that you may be filled with all the fullness of God.*

Now to Him who is able to do exceedingly abundantly above all that we ask or think, according to the power that works in us.

Ephesians 3:17–20, emphasis added

The author of Hebrews says:

> But *without faith it is impossible to please Him*,
> for he who comes to God must believe that He is,
> and that He is a rewarder of those who diligently
> seek Him.　　　Hebrews 11:6, emphasis added

*Once you are firmly persuaded of God's goodness
and love for you, that His desire is to fill you with His
fullness and that He will in fact reward your efforts in
seeking Him, there will be no more hesitation.*

Hesitation says that you are not sure of God's love and motives. As time passes, hesitation causes doubt, and the enemy uses your doubts to draw you away. Paul mentions several times in His letters that he is "persuaded," and we have to become the same:

> I was appointed a preacher, an apostle, and a
> teacher of the Gentiles. For this reason I also
> suffer these things; nevertheless I am not
> ashamed, for I know whom I have believed and
> *am persuaded* that He is able to keep what I
> have committed to Him until that Day.
> 　　　　　2 Timothy 1:11–12, emphasis added

By becoming fully convinced that what God promises He is also able and desirous to perform (see Romans 4:21), Paul was able to say:

> For *I am persuaded* that neither death nor life,
> nor angels nor principalities nor powers, nor
> things present nor things to come, nor height
> nor depth, nor any other created thing, shall be
> able to separate us from the love of God which
> is in Christ Jesus our Lord.   Romans 8:38–39

Hesitation, in some instances, can cost us the victory. God wants us to become finely tuned and well-trained kingdom professionals. It could be damaging should we hesitate during an important moment of our earthly training. Remember, God wants you to succeed, not fail.

During pilot training, I learned the cost of hesitation. At cruising altitude, an airplane is traveling approximately 600 miles an hour, which is 10 miles a minute. Cruising altitude is about forty thousand feet, or almost eight miles above the ground. Because of the airplane's speed and height, the pilot must begin descent to his destination at least one hundred miles out. By hesitating for even one minute for any reason, he could overfly the airport by ten miles. In addition, being only one degree off the course heading during a two-hour flight puts the aircraft more than one hundred miles off course from its destination.

I trained in martial arts to learn techniques for disarming a person before they could fire their weapon. These techniques must be performed quickly without hesitation. Hesitating means you must go to plan B, which is surrendering to the enemy.

The point is that *faith* means "being firmly convinced." Faith causes us to react with our objective in mind. Having genuine faith takes us where the Spirit of God wants to take us because it eliminates hesitation and distractions that would take us off course from our spiritual objective. Faith is being firmly convinced of what we believe and in whom we believe.

*If your faith is solid, without hesitation, then during final approach to your spiritual objective, you can be accurate and on time in reaching your prize. And, when the enemy comes to intimidate and distract you, you do not hesitate, but disarm him and send him away with a mission failure.*

# Chapter 8

# Knockin' on Heaven's Door

As Jesus taught me wonderful truths about Him and His kingdom, I realized how fortunate I was that He had given me so much time out of His busy schedule (almost an hour). Awed by His love and desire to help me, I realized that no one on earth can give love as He does. We of the earth realm are more self-centered, and our first reaction is usually selfish. Jesus, however, is never selfish. He doesn't need anything, and He just wants to give us what He has.

*Jesus wants your fellowship because He created you. He yearns for you to talk with Him about your thoughts and concerns. Jesus always has a way out of every situation. Take His hand and allow Him to guide you to your next step. You are so close to your next miracle. He has brought you to a place where only He can deliver you; the supernatural lies just ahead. Your provision is on the other side of your mountain. Yield to the supernatural and speak to your mountain (see Mark 11:23–24).*

## A GRAVE DISAPPOINTMENT

I was waiting for Jesus to take me to the heavenly city to meet all the people who had gone before me, including my heroes from the Old and New Testaments. Then I received very disappointing news: He told me I was going back to my life on earth.

This was unacceptable to me. After spending almost an hour with Jesus, I felt comfortable enough with Him to voice my displeasure of His decision. I began to argue my case in rapid, and what I thought were eloquent and convincing, statements. I reminded Him of how slow the earth realm was to respond when I prayed. It often took many weeks to receive an answer. Even though the answer was sent immediately, warfare with Satan's kingdom caused a lengthy delay.

I reminded Him that the presence of rebellious spirits (demons) was prevalent around people, influencing them to rebel against God. I told Him that much of what I had experienced on the earth, in the area of spiritual warfare, was due to the outside influence of evil spirits coming against me and not from wrong motives of my heart . I thought my reasons were persuasive as I explained why I should not return. My arguments seemed convincing to me, so I rested my case.

I expected Him to change His mind and take me home to the city of God. Instead, He smiled gently and said, "Kevin, you're not going back for yourself. You are returning for all these people." Then He pointed to the far wall of the operating room and continued: "You are going back to minister to the people I'm sending you to. You had finished your race today, but I am sending you back on a mission to talk to them. Their lives will be rerouted because I sent you to them, and they will be changed. They will never be the same. It's all extra credit."

Looking to where He pointed, I saw many people standing against the wall; in fact, I couldn't see an end to the line. About twenty-five people were immediately visible. (As I write, I have met over one hundred of the people Jesus sent me back to speak with.)

He continued: "When you come in contact with one of these people, you will recall this visitation; and I will come, stand by your side, and speak into your right ear." He demonstrated this by standing beside me and whispering in my right ear. "Just repeat word for word what I say, and their lives will be changed forever," He continued. "Everything is extra credit because you have finished your race and completed all I have ever asked of you." He further encouraged me by telling me that I would not fail and made me understand that I could not lose. Everything was to be gained, and I would have sure success as I closely followed Him.

## DIVINE ASSIGNMENTS

Many of the people I saw during my heavenly visitation have since been touched by Jesus in the earthly realm as His supernatural visitation interrupted their natural life. My heavenly appointments with the first twenty-five people were shown to me in the supernatural during my operation. We must ask the Lord for understanding of our ultimate and immediate purpose during our time in this earthly realm because . . .

> *God has plans for your future, and you need to align yourself with them; they are your divine appointments. If you want to be included in supernatural events, then make yourself ready—by believing everything written in the Bible and being ready to say no to fleshly appetites and your will, and yes to His Spirit and His will. His way is always the best way. God has an appointment book filled with supernatural events with your name penciled next to them.*

When you do not make a divine appointment you were scheduled for, it is called a "missed appointment." That's where the word "dis-appointment" comes from. In heaven, there are no dis-appointments—God has only completed appointments. Decide to believe this truth, and stand, in Jesus' name, against every evil spirit that works against you. No more missed appointments and thus no more disappointments.

## BACK TO MY BODY

As Jesus was wrapping up His teaching, I began sensing my body, which was still on the operating table, pulling to reconnect with my spirit man. While Jesus was still talking, I felt something in my mouth. We were standing a distance from the operating table, so this puzzled me. Then I felt someone pull an object out of my mouth, and Jesus noticed that I was puzzled. He said, "You are going back to your body now, and you will wake up, so I must leave." What I felt was the doctor and nurse removing cotton and the structure they had been placed in my mouth to hold it open during the procedure. The operation was complete.

Jesus started walking to the place where He had appeared initially, the door with immense glory coming through it. It was so bright that I could hardly look at it directly. The door was a foot off the ground and at least one foot shorter than Jesus. He ducked and stepped through. Seeing Him leave was the hardest thing I have ever endured. I wanted to go with Him so badly. Also, I had a question that I had not asked because He had been talking the entire time. I was very disappointed about missing my chance to get this important question answered.

At that precise moment, He heard my thoughts and stuck His head back through the door and answered my question. His response to this personal question was important to me since I was going back to earth. Then immediately I was sucked back into my body on the operating table and woke up weeping. I did not want to return, but at least Jesus had answered my very important question. However, I could not stop crying as they pushed me into the recovery area.

## EVERYTHING COUNTS

I want to discuss another insight that Jesus gave me that can help you accomplish all He has planned for you. He wants you to fulfill every word that is written about you in your book (see Psalm 139:16). Some truths might be hard to accept at first, but they are necessary for success. First, everything we do in obedience to His Word counts in heaven. Also, everything we do in His name—even things that seem insignificant, like giving a sandwich to someone—will not go unrewarded (see Mark 9:41).

*Nothing is insignificant to the Lord. We are to be obedient to everything He tells us in His Word and by the Holy Spirit speaking to our hearts.*

After graduating from college in 1985, I attended a two-year program to prepare for the ministry. However, upon graduation from this program, the Lord led me to seek employment with Southwest Airlines. A vision in 1986 showed that I would be hired by Southwest in two years. Two years later, in the exact month that I had the vision, I was in fact hired. During the first five years of my employment with the airline, I fed the homeless and talked to people about Jesus in many cities where I spent the night.

In the second week of December in 1999, I was in Burbank, California, and did my usual thing, which was to leave the hotel after check-in to get something to eat. During my return to the hotel, I walked through a busy commercial area and ran across a homeless person, who was turned away from me and covered in blankets. This person, who I thought might be a woman, had the usual shopping cart overflowing with belongings. I had no food to give, so I asked the Lord silently what I should do. I heard the Lord say, "Give her twenty dollars." I obeyed, but reluctantly, because I was saving money for my wife's Christmas present, and I never gave cash to homeless people, for obvious reasons.

When I approached her, I was not prepared for what happened next. I spoke loudly to get her attention, and when she turned to me, I handed her the money. I could not see her face because of the blankets draped over her head. When she pulled the blankets back, I saw she had bright blue eyes and appeared to be a woman.

I told her that God loved her and that He wanted her to have this money. She quickly responded, "You have done what the Lord has asked you to do, and I was sent to warn you that hard times are coming to America. God wants you to prepare and be careful with every dollar and to use them wisely." Finished talking, she handed me back my money. Stunned by the message and the messenger, I wondered who she was, because homeless people do not prophesy or return twenty-dollar bills, especially at Christmastime.

Having turned to walk away, I thought, "I'll ask her name". Less than two-seconds had passed before I turned back to find that she was gone; even her cart had disappeared. She had been only two feet away. I looked in every direction. In a matter of seconds, she would have had to travel a hundred feet to disappear from sight.

Because of that angelic word, I took my money out of the stock market. Within five months of the visitation, the market began to crash and fluctuate wildly, but my money was safe. After the market dip of September 11, 2001, I was really glad the angel had warned me, because my losses were minimal. By February of 2002, I had fully reinvested. The funds in which I reinvested had fallen between 60 percent and 80 percent before I got back into the market. I rode the funds up as the markets improved, until July of 2008. Unknown to me, this was the top of the market, and I would soon receive another warning.

## THE SMALL THINGS

While seated with my wife in the Seattle airport, I had another visitation. This time I felt as if someone came to stand by me as the Holy Spirit surrounded me. Then the word of the Lord came, saying, "It's time to get out. The markets are going to crash again." That was July 2008, and I had sensed something was wrong with the economy. Now I knew it was time to act. I responded immediately and got online with my laptop, and within ten minutes, I had cashed out of my investments.

By the end of September 2008, the markets were falling again, but I did not lose a penny. The following spring, I reinvested into the funds that I had previously owned. They had again lost between 60 percent and 80 percent. The market returned to higher levels by 2013, and I successfully rode the market back up for the second time.

Because of the heavenly warnings, for the past nine years I have been in the market only during the upturns and not during the downturns. I now have over four times my original investment because of the angelic warnings. Obviously, this would be impossible without heaven's help. But it doesn't end there; I have had more financial warnings that I will discuss in future books.

I was curious why the Lord told me about the two major market crashes and a third one that is to come, but did not disclose it to the professionals involved in the economy. I don't know of anyone who predicted both the 2001 and 2008 market crashes. So I decided to return to Burbank, California, to thank the Lord for what He had done for me.

I went to the spot where the angel had appeared as a street person. Holding the printout of my retirement portfolio, I stood in a moment of silence on that spot. I thanked God for quadrupling my investments and asked why He had been so gracious to me. In the silence, I heard these words clearly: "I kept track of every sandwich you gave to a poor person, and I was just paying you back." Night after night for five years, I did that for Him, and He remembered that small thing.

*Take care of His business and He will take care of yours—everything counts!*

## RETURNED FOR A REASON

Back to my encounter with Jesus: Within a few weeks of my return to life, I started meeting the individuals Jesus had introduced to me during our time together. I recognized many of them. Each time I met one, Jesus came and stood on my right side and whispered into my right ear what His heart was for that particular person. I would sense the supernatural realm as destiny surrounded us, and for a timeless moment, we would bask in the presence of Jesus the Messiah. Many were saved or returned to God, and others were encouraged by what happened as we participated in that supernatural event. I sense the Lord will bring even more people to me for help.

Jesus continues to visit me, and the realm of the supernatural is becoming more dominant each day. Every day is a gift I am thankful for. I could be in heaven now, but instead I have been sent back to help people become ready for the Lord's return.

*Walk in His truth, expect His power, and the Lord will take you places you never dreamed of going.*

# Chapter 9

# Discerning the Time of *Your* Visitation

❧

Whether you know it or not, God is visiting you right now. By His infinite wisdom and foresight, He planned for you to come to the knowledge and understanding of who He is, what He has done for you through Jesus Christ, and what He wants to do for you and through you *now*. If you are "in Him," you stand before Him holy, blameless, and in His love (see Ephesians 1:4). If you haven't committed your life to Him, then now is the time to do so.

As a child of God, you have a specific purpose and a personal mission. That makes it vital for you to receive information and instruction about God's plan for your life. This occurs at a time called your "visitation," and you can expect to have more than one.

*Discerning the time of your visitation will activate you in your supernatural assignment and reveal spiritual truths important to your mission and life on earth.*

Missing the time of your visitation can be disastrous, as Jerusalem learned:

> Now as He [Jesus] drew near, He saw the city [Jerusalem] and wept over it, saying, "If you had known, even you, especially in this your day, the things that make for your peace! But now they are hidden from your eyes. For days will come upon you when your enemies will build an embankment around you, surround you and close you in on every side, and level you, and your children within you, to the ground; and they will not leave in you one stone upon another, because *you did not know the time of your visitation.*" (emphasis added)

## A MARITAL VISITATION

One evening during the first week of January in 1993, I was on my way home from church after music practice in Phoenix, Arizona, when my car filled with a strong presence of heaven. It was as though someone straight from heaven were sitting in the passenger's seat beside me. Then I heard what seemed to me an audible voice say, "You are going to Seattle this weekend, and you are going to meet your wife." I had never been to Seattle and did not know anyone who lived there. The visitation in my car ended when I arrived at the house where I was staying.

The lady I was house-sitting for was at home when I arrived and greeted me at the door. The presence of God was still on me, and she sensed that something supernatural had just happened to me. I told her that God had just spoken to me and I needed to pray. When we sat down to pray, the presence I felt while in my car showed up again, and we had an amazing time of prayer.

It was wonderful because heaven came into that house and the glory rested on us. I then mentioned that God told me that I was going to Seattle and would meet my wife-to-be that weekend. She began to laugh and said, "I happen to be going to Seattle to visit someone this weekend, too, and I already know who your wife is. I have known her for a while. I believe she is the right one because every time I'm with her, I think of you. I will pick you up at the airport when you arrive and introduce you to several women at church on Sunday. But I will not tell you who I think is to be your wife; I'll let God do that."

That weekend I flew up to Seattle. When I walked into the church on Sunday, my eyes immediately fell on Kathi, and I heard the Lord say, "There she is!" After service, I met her, along with a number of other single women who attended the church. Later my friend asked me which one was to be my wife. I told her that it was Kathi, and she said, "Yes, she is the one I had in mind for you." We laughed and pondered how this would unfold.

Later, in February, I returned to Seattle to ask Kathi for a date. On the fifth of February, we had our first date, and it was also our hour of visitation. The same presence that had come into my car and the house where I lived showed up again and stood by our table at the restaurant. We were immediately covered with the presence of heaven. We sat there and wept, but we never took a bite of our food while God confirmed to each of us our future union. We had our meals boxed up and gave them to a street person on the way to the car. Eight days later, on the thirteenth of February, we were engaged; and on May 8 of that year, we were married in Selah, Washington, by four minister friends who believe in the supernatural.

Over the years, we have had many times of visitation when we were overwhelmed by heaven's presence as we perhaps entertained angels unaware. Only a few weeks prior to this writing, our bedroom filled with the presence of God so strong that we could not have stood if we had tried. It lasted for some time as God confirmed His destiny in our lives.

Don't miss the day of your visitation; it will alter your life!

# Conclusion

I want you to fully understand the life-changing nature of my visitation with Jesus. I am not the same person I was before that experience. I have gained much wisdom and understanding from the Lord about what goes on behind the scenes in the spirit realm.

I learned that you can trust the accuracy of the Word of God. I now realize you can take God's Word at face value, like a child would. As I continue to grow in the Lord, He gives me increasing revelation of His ways. I have found myself caught up in the counsel of God, privy to behind-the-scenes discussions about present and future events and other things.

There is so much more to Father God than we know and can learn in this lifetime and even through all eternity. More and more, I find myself yielding to the Holy Spirit without resistance because of my realization that He can take me farther in the direction I am to go than I could ever do myself. I feel a sense of destiny every day as the mysteries of Jesus' life, purpose, and perfect will are increasingly being unfolded. Even while writing this book, I was visited again by the same presence of God that I encountered more than twenty-two years ago.

I believe that you, the reader, can receive a supernatural impartation from heaven as you read the pages of this book. I know the Lord wants you to benefit from my story of being sent back from heaven. You cannot imagine what can happen to you if you will decide to yield to the Holy Spirit without qualm, preconceived notions, or resistance. I know that when I finally go to heaven permanently, I will see the faithfulness of the Lord in the people's lives He somehow touched through me—lives redirected and changed forever. God also wants to do that for you.

You cannot go beyond your understanding of something. You will always encounter limits when your understanding of a subject runs out. But when you train yourself to always be receptive to the flow of revelation from God's Word and His presence, you will find the limitations are taken off.

*There is such liberty and deliverance when you finally let the Holy Spirit be your guide. I have seen the lives of hundreds of people changed by the ministry of the Holy Spirit as He orchestrated their divine appointments.*

May God bless you as you pursue Him with all your heart, and may you have your own time of supernatural visitation.

# Author's Note

Please look for the companion study guide that will be offered in the near future for personal and group Bible studies.

Lightning Source UK Ltd.
Milton Keynes UK
UKHW021923260819
348660UK00015B/882/P